THE POCKET CHINESE ASTROLOGY

Published in 2025
by Gemini Books
Part of Gemini Books Group

Based in Woodbridge and London

Marine House, Tide Mill Way
Woodbridge, Suffolk IP12 1AP
United Kingdom
www.geminibooks.com

Text and Design © 2025 Gemini Adult Books Ltd
Part of the Gemini Pockets series

Cover image: Prachaya Roekdeethaweesab/Shutterstock.com
Text by Becky Miles

ISBN 978-1-78675-178-2

All rights reserved. No part of this publication may be reproduced in any form or by any means – electronic, mechanical, photocopying, recording or otherwise – or stored in any retrieval system of any nature without prior written permission from the copyright holders.

A CIP catalogue record for this book is available from the British Library.

Disclaimer: The book is a guidebook purely for information and entertainment purposes only. All trademarks, individual and company names, brand names, registered names, quotations, celebrity names, logos, dialogues and catchphrases used or cited in this book are the property of their respective owners. The publisher does not assume and hereby disclaims any liability to any party for any loss, damage or disruption caused by errors or omissions, whether such errors or omissions result from negligence, accident or any other cause. This book is an unofficial and unauthorized publication by Gemini Books Ltd and has not been licensed, approved, sponsored or endorsed by any person or entity.

Printed in China

10 9 8 7 6 5 4 3 2 1

Images: Shutterstock.com: jennylipets 8; kotoffei 7, 27; Luis Line 56, 62, 68, 74, 80, 86, 92, 98, 104, 110, 116, 122; Sarunyo_foto 8, 22, 36; StockSmartStart 17-21; Tasefa design 4; Wise ant 29; Zaie 52, 58, 60, 64, 66, 70, 72, 76, 78, 82, 84, 88, 90, 94, 96, 100, 102, 106, 108, 112, 114, 118, 120, 124, 126.

THE POCKET

CHINESE ASTROLOGY

G:

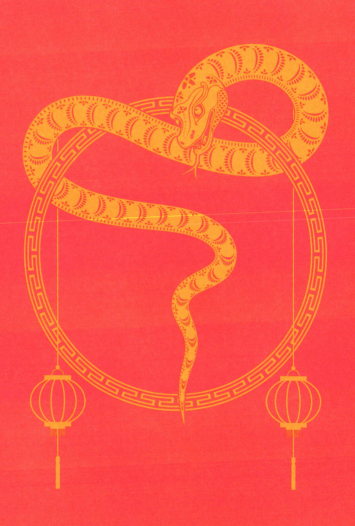

CONTENTS

Introduction 6

CHAPTER ONE
The Chinese Year 9

CHAPTER TWO
Guiding Principles 23

CHAPTER THREE
The Five Elements 37

CHAPTER FOUR
The 12 Animal Signs 53

Introduction

The Chinese zodiac comprises 12 animal signs rotating in a 12-yearly cycle, with your own sign being determined by your birth year.

The signs are: Rat, Ox, Tiger, Rabbit, Monkey, Dragon, Snake, Horse, Goat, Rooster, Dog and Pig.

Each sign has its own archetypal traits, which are further influenced by the five key elements of Chinese tradition – Water, Earth, Wood, Fire and Metal – as well as by the animals that preside over the month and hour of your birth.

Read on to discover more about your own character through the signs and elements – and their interactions with each other.

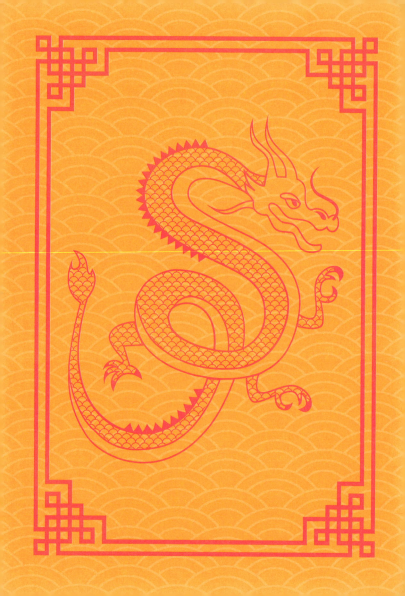

Chapter One

THE CHINESE YEAR

CHINESE ASTROLOGY

The lunar calendar

Chinese astrology is based on
the traditional Chinese lunar calendar,
which dates back more than 4,500 years.

Although the Western Gregorian calendar
has been in common use in China for over
a hundred years, the lunar calendar still
holds sway culturally, and it is this system
that dictates the beginning of a new year,
and new animal, in the Chinese zodiac.

THE CHINESE YEAR

Chinese New Year

The first day of the Chinese lunar year – commonly called Chinese New Year or the Spring Festival – is usually the second new moon after the winter solstice and the closest new moon to the start of spring.

CHINESE ASTROLOGY

The New Year dates

Chinese New Year falls on a different
date between 21 January and 20 February
each year. The dates for the zodiac differ
slightly each year accordingly, and
you can check the dates of your
specific sign and birth
year in Chapter Four.

THE CHINESE YEAR

2,000 years ago

Celebrations for Chinese New Year are thought to date back to the 14th century BCE, but the date was first fixed as the first day of the new lunar year during the Han dynasty, around 2,000 years ago.

Celebrating the new year

Festivities begin with the new moon and last for two weeks, when the full moon appears.

This holiday is the biggest in the Chinese calendar, as families gather to honour their ancestors and to usher in the new year with its promise of renewal, new energy and good luck.

Feasts are prepared, red lanterns are hung in the streets and in people's homes, and the new year itself is welcomed in with huge firework displays, the setting off of firecrackers, and parades featuring lion and dragon dances.

And with the new year, attention turns to the new zodiac animal and the influences it will bring to bear, not only on those born in one of its years but on all of the signs and how they relate to one other.

> "Yin and yang take turns. The four seasons come and go. The moon waxes and wanes. All things have their time."

Wang Anshi

CHINESE ASTROLOGY

The origin of the animals

In Chinese mythology, the Jade Emperor, who had ruled the heavens for many years, wanted some of Earth's creatures to guard the Heavenly Gate and help him measure time. He decreed they should compete in a race, which included crossing a fast-flowing river, to determine the order of animals in the new 12-yearly zodiac.

THE CHINESE YEAR

The Rat and the Ox

The cunning Rat persuaded the good-natured Ox to let it catch a ride across the river on the Ox's head. When they both got to the safety of the bank, the Rat jumped down and darted across the finish line to win the race.

This earned the Rat first place in the zodiac, with the Ox coming second.

CHINESE ASTROLOGY

The Tiger, the Rabbit and the Dragon

The Tiger came third, after battling the strong currents that had sent him off course.

Fourth was the clever Rabbit, who had managed to scramble onto a floating log.

Fifth was the Dragon, who – after saving some nearby villagers by putting out a fire! – had kindly blown a puff of wind to help the Rabbit across.

The Snake and the Horse

The Horse thought it had made sixth place, but hadn't noticed the Snake wrapped around one of its hooves.

The Snake slithered off the Horse just before the finish line, coming in sixth while the Horse was seventh.

CHINESE ASTROLOGY

The Goat, the Monkey and the Rooster

Eighth, ninth and tenth spots were given to the Goat, the Monkey and the Rooster respectively, who had banded together to navigate the rushing waters on a raft.

The Dog and the Pig

Eleventh was the Dog who, while a strong swimmer, had been having so much fun splashing around in the river that ten creatures overtook it.

Lastly, the Pig took twelfth position after stopping to eat, and then take a nap, along the way.

Chapter Two
GUIDING PRINCIPLES

A holistic view

Understanding Chinese astrology and what it means for you involves more than simply looking at the traits associated with the animal of your birth year.

Taking a holistic view of your horoscope, and considering different aspects that influence you, gives you the tools to learn about yourself, to discover patterns and inclinations, and can guide you in future decision-making.

GUIDING PRINCIPLES

Influences on the zodiac

As well as the year of your birth, your Chinese horoscope is influenced by:

- The concept of yin and yang
- The signs that relate to your time and month of birth
- The five elements (in Chapter Three)
- Your own personal circumstances, including your family and where you live
- The sign that governs the present year.

Studying the traits that each animal, element and yin or yang influence add to your main zodiac animal's characteristics will help you develop insights into your own Chinese horoscope.

CHINESE ASTROLOGY

Yin and yang

Originating in Chinese philosophy, the concept of yin and yang describes how all things exist in an interconnected, self-perpetuating cycle of opposing but complementary forces.

These forces, or energies, are to be kept in a state of balance for optimal harmony in our lives.

GUIDING PRINCIPLES

Yin is the passive, dark, female principle of the universe, while yang represents the active, light, male principle.

Each of the 12 signs of the Chinese zodiac are designated as either a yin or yang sign, but this is not to say that your sign is thought to embody yin or yang traits exclusively.

Rather, their influences are another strand to consider when seeking to understand your sign's characteristics and how they relate to your life, relationships and possible compatibility with others.

Yin signs

Ox
Rabbit
Snake
Goat
Rooster
Pig

Yang signs

Rat
Tiger
Dragon
Horse
Monkey
Dog

The month and hour of birth

Each of the 12 lunar months
of the year is presided over by
one of the animal signs, as is each of
12 two-hour periods in the 24-hour day.
So, it is possible that you were born
in a Dragon month, in a Dragon year,
at a time of day also governed by the
Dragon sign – a lot of Dragon, indeed!

More likely is that you have at least one,
probably two, different signs interacting
with your birth year sign to create
a combination of influences and
characteristics for you to explore.

> **May you be as vigorous as dragons and horses, and may you enjoy great fortune.**

Traditional Chinese New Year greeting

CHINESE ASTROLOGY

Month of birth

The lunar months are slightly different to those in the western calendar – dictated by the new moon. Therefore, the exact dates do vary slightly each year, so if you are on the cusp, check the year's dates with a Chinese almanac.

Their dates and associated Chinese zodiac animals are as follows:

GUIDING PRINCIPLES

21 January – 19 February: **Tiger**
20 February – 20 March: **Rabbit**
21 March – 19 April: **Dragon**
20 April – 20 May: **Snake**
21 May – 21 June: **Horse**
22 June – 21 July: **Goat**
22 July – 21 August: **Monkey**
22 August – 22 September: **Rooster**
23 September – 22 October: **Dog**
23 October – 21 November: **Pig**
22 November – 21 December: **Rat**
22 December – 20 January: **Ox**

CHINESE ASTROLOGY

Hour of birth

In ancient times, the zodiac was used to
tell the time. Each animal represented a two-hour
period, designated by specific traits.

For example, the Tiger hunts for prey
in the early morning hours, and the
Horse is awake and lively at midday,
when many animals are resting.

The signs that influence you
according to your hour of
birth are ordered as follows:

GUIDING PRINCIPLES

1am – 3am: **Ox**
3am – 5am: **Tiger**
5am – 7am: **Rabbit**
7am – 9am: **Dragon**
9am – 11am: **Snake**
11am – 1pm: **Horse**
1pm – 3pm: **Goat**
3pm – 5pm: **Monkey**
5pm – 7pm: **Rooster**
7pm – 9pm: **Dog**
9pm – 11pm: **Pig**
11pm – 1am: **Rat**

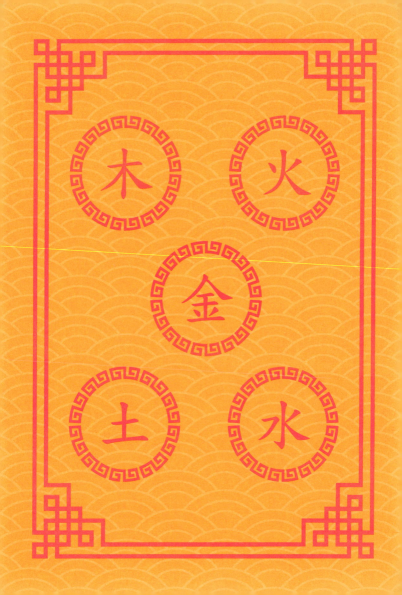

Chapter Three

THE FIVE ELEMENTS

CHINESE ASTROLOGY

The elements

In Chinese tradition, the five elements describe the basic energetic qualities of everything in the universe. Each one has its own attributes and is also linked to a season of the year. They are:

• **Water – birth year ending 2 or 3**

• **Earth – birth year ending 8 or 9**

• **Wood – birth year ending 4 or 5**

• **Fire – birth year ending 6 or 7**

• **Metal – birth year ending 0 or 1**

THE FIVE ELEMENTS

Your birth year element

Each element exerts influence over birth years ending in one of two numbers.

For example, Water element characteristics are associated with years ending in a 2 or 3.

So, if you were born in 1983 – the year of the Pig – you are a Water Pig, and if you were born in 2002 – the year of the Horse – you are a Water Horse.

As such, with 12 zodiac animals and five influencing elements, this gives a 60-year cycle, whereby a Water Pig, Fire Snake or any other combination would only be born every 60 years.

CHINESE ASTROLOGY

Your fixed element

As well as considering the element associated with the year of your actual birth, each zodiacal sign also has a "fixed" element that impacts your horoscope.

The fixed element for the Horse is Fire, so if you were born in 2002 – the year of the Horse – your variable element is Water (you are a Water Horse) but your fixed element is Fire, and both exert influence.

And if you were born in a year where the fixed and variable element is one and the same, you have double the influence of its characteristics.

THE FIVE ELEMENTS

Your associated elements

When looking at your Chinese horoscope as a whole, be sure to take into account the characteristics of your associated elements – your birth year element and your fixed element, as well as those characteristics that describe the zodiac animal from the year of your birth.

CHINESE ASTROLOGY

Water

Influences birth years ending in 2 or 3

SEASON:
Winter

AUSPICIOUS COLOURS:
Black, Grey

FIXED ELEMENT OF:
Rat, Pig

THE FIVE ELEMENTS

Water has a flowing and moulding energy, and this element is most often related to creativity and sensitivity. Its associated season is winter, when it might cover the ground in frost or freeze in a lake, with everything quietly at rest underneath, waiting for the spring.

Water signs can be reflective, imaginative and persuasive, but also value social interaction and family connection. They can be gentle like a stream and strong-willed like the sea, and working to balance these two energies is important.

Earth

Influences birth years ending in 8 or 9

SEASON:
Transitional weeks between the seasons

AUSPICIOUS COLOURS:
Yellow, Gold

FIXED ELEMENT OF:
Ox, Dragon, Goat, Dog

THE FIVE ELEMENTS

The Earth element offers stability in times of transition, as well as abundance, nurturing and nourishment.

With sharp focus and a strong dedication to their goals, Earth types are also thoughtful, kind and honest, calm and reliable.

Often peacemakers, they need to balance their desire to help with patience, and must remember to take time for themselves to avoid energetic depletion.

CHINESE ASTROLOGY

Wood

Influences birth years ending in 4 or 5

SEASON:
Spring

AUSPICIOUS COLOURS:
Green, Blue

FIXED ELEMENT OF:
Tiger, Rabbit

Wood energy signals life and growth –
aspects synonymous with spring.
As saplings grow into strong trees,
this element moves resolutely forwards,
pushing obstacles out of its path.

Wood signs are enthusiastic and
practical, warm and friendly. However,
they are also idealistic and competitive,
which can sometimes lead to frustration.

Their boldness and strength of character,
reminiscent of a towering oak, need to be
tempered with the flexibility of the young
sapling to achieve a harmonious balance.

Fire

Influences birth years ending in 6 or 7

SEASON:
Summer

AUSPICIOUS COLOURS:
Red, Purple

FIXED ELEMENT OF:
Snake, Horse

THE FIVE ELEMENTS

Allied with summer – the season of warmth, activity and growth – those born in a Fire year are passionate, generous and resilient.

Also gifted with sensuality and spontaneity, their direct manner and emotional intensity can sometimes leave them vulnerable to jealousy and burnout. Balancing this with time out for self-care, especially in nature, is important.

CHINESE ASTROLOGY

Metal

Influences birth years ending in 0 or 1

SEASON:
Autumn

AUSPICIOUS COLOURS:
White, Silver

FIXED ELEMENT OF:
Monkey, Rooster

THE FIVE ELEMENTS

The Metal element gives solid and determined energy. Linked to autumn, strength and steadiness are required to move through the changes that this season brings as the natural world dies back in preparation for the rest of winter ahead of the return of spring.

Focused and disciplined, Metal types are also loyal friends, although they could work on tempering their determination with some flexibility and on a willingness to embrace change.

Chapter Four
THE 12 ANIMAL SIGNS

CHINESE ASTROLOGY

Working with your sign

This chapter explores each sign in more detail, describing main character traits, compatibility in relationships, career and health prospects, and how your animal year can influence other signs in the zodiac.

Each sign is also linked with related colours and numbers, which may be auspicious or hold particular resonance for you.

THE 12 ANIMAL SIGNS

Remember that no animal sign is inherently better or worse than any other. All have a range of characteristics – both positive and negative – and different elements, traits and circumstances can all be influenced by each other.

You have agency in how you choose to work with your personal horoscope and qualities. As with all things in Chinese philosophy, striving for balance is key to living a good life.

The Rat

RAT YEARS

10 February 1948 – 28 January 1949: **Earth**

28 January 1960 – 14 February 1961: **Metal**

15 February 1972 – 2 February 1973: **Water**

2 February 1984 – 19 February 1985: **Wood**

19 February 1996 – 6 February 1997: **Fire**

7 February 2008 – 25 January 2009: **Earth**

25 January 2020 – 11 February 2021: **Metal**

11 February 2032 – 30 January 2033: **Water**

COLOURS: Blue, Gold, Green

NUMBERS: 2 and 3

FIXED ELEMENT: Water

Traits

The first sign of the zodiac, the Rat is a sociable, charming, creative and resourceful creature.

Quick-witted and kind, Rats are good at taking opportunities and making money (sometimes to the point of greed), and while they can be cautious lenders, they are generous to family and friends.

Rats are ambitious and adaptable, but must take care not to get distracted with endless new projects as they race through life.

Relationships

The charming and flirtatious Rat gets (and loves) a lot of attention from admirers. Their sensual, passionate nature is most compatible with Monkeys or Dragons, who share their creative and energetic qualities.

Rats are least compatible with Horses, with whom they tend to clash in romantic relationships.

As well as their friends, family is very important to the Rat, as a nurturing and supportive force in their life.

Career

Rats are smart and meticulous and usually possess keen judgment. Serious about their work, they do well in jobs that require excellent communication skills and firm decision-making, such as administrator, entrepreneur, writer, journalist, politician, lawyer, banker, counsellor, researcher or musician.

Ambitious and hard-working, they instinctively know how to get ahead and prefer being in charge, trusting in their superior ability to problem-solve.

Health

The busy, active Rat must not ignore any signs of stress or overdoing it, and be sure to build time for rest and relaxation into their schedule.

As a Water sign, the kidneys and urinary system are key, so maintaining good hydration is important.

The gregarious Rat can be fond of rich food and prone to over-indulgence, which is not best helped by fast-paced physical activity. Gentler pursuits, such as tai chi or yoga, will achieve balance here.

Influence over other signs

As the first zodiac sign, any Year of the Rat is seen as a good time for new beginnings, new projects and new ideas.

Its strong energy can be unsettling for signs that don't suit a gung-ho approach, so remember to be gentle with yourself if this is you.

The Ox

OX YEARS

29 January 1949 – 15 February 1950: **Earth**
15 February 1961 – 4 February 1962: **Metal**
3 February 1973 – 23 January 1974: **Water**
20 February 1985 – 8 February 1986: **Wood**
7 February 1997 – 27 January 1998: **Fire**
26 January 2009 – 13 February 2010: **Earth**
12 February 2021 – 31 January 2022: **Metal**
31 January 2033 – 18 February 2034: **Water**

COLOURS: White, Yellow, Green

NUMBERS: 1 and 4

FIXED ELEMENT: Earth

Traits

Patient, hard-working and determined, the Ox is a resolute character whose honesty and dependability makes for a loyal friend.

Their methodical approach to life helps them work successfully toward their goals, but with this single-mindedness can come a degree of inflexibility.

Strong and self-sufficient, the Ox is not always a lover of authority, especially if this goes against their careful plans, and while generally calm, an Ox provoked can be a dangerous creature.

Relationships

The Ox's key trait of dependability makes for a faithful partner, once they have weighed up all considerations and decided to commit.

Often quiet and introverted, security and reliability are important to the Ox and they can be deeply hurt by any betrayal, be this in romantic, platonic or familial relationships.

They are best matched with Snakes and Roosters, who share their purposeful approach to life, and least compatible with the sometimes equally stubborn Goat.

THE 12 ANIMAL SIGNS

Career

Conscientious, organized and practical, the hard-working Ox enjoys work that has a strong element of routine and requires an eye for detail.

As such, they do well in jobs in teaching, engineering, banking and pharmacy.

With Earth as their fixed element, careers in farming and horticulture are also excellent options.

Health

Having the "constitution of an ox" is an apt saying for this sign, and the Ox is a generally healthy and robust creature. However, there is a need to balance their immense capacity for hard work with restful breaks and regular exercise.

The associated organs of Earth signs are the stomach and digestive system, and Oxen should pay particular attention to variety in their diet, especially if they lead a mostly sedentary life, rather than over-relying on their familiar favourites.

THE 12 ANIMAL SIGNS

Influence over other signs

An Ox year is a good time for laying down firm foundations and steadily working toward one's goals and, with a degree of patience, you will see clear progress.

Impatient risk-takers would be advised to take a breath and do their homework before embarking on new projects.

The Tiger

TIGER YEARS

16 February 1950 – 5 February 1951: **Metal**

5 February 1962 – 24 January 1963: **Water**

24 January 1974 – 10 February 1975: **Wood**

9 February 1986 – 28 January 1987: **Fire**

28 January 1998 – 15 February 1999: **Earth**

14 February 2010 – 2 February 2011: **Metal**

1 February 2022 – 21 January 2023: **Water**

19 February 2034 – 7 February 2035: **Wood**

COLOURS: Blue, Grey, Orange

NUMBERS: 1, 3 and 4

FIXED ELEMENT: Wood

THE 12 ANIMAL SIGNS

Traits

Confident and courageous, the Tiger is hard-working and bold, all the while loving attention and more than a little drama!

With their fearlessness comes an element of unpredictability and sometimes risky decision-making, but the captivating Tiger is a force of nature that usually succeeds in the end.

Whether adventurous or restless for change, Tigers make good leaders and are not afraid to make tough calls, but would be advised to seek the wisdom of others before making a big leap.

Relationships

Passionate and romantic, Tigers are best partnered with signs that share their sense of adventure – they can struggle if they feel tied down.

Most compatible with Dogs and Horses, Tigers can clash with Monkeys and Snakes.

While they may have a wide social circle on the surface, the Tiger likes to be in control and can be hard to get to know well. If you can keep up with them, they are generous and big-hearted, but their desire to roam free can make this difficult.

Career

Creative and influential leaders and entrepreneurs, Tigers are best suited to fast-paced, exciting jobs and will not find fulfilment in repetitive or mundane work.

Their competitive nature suits a career in sales and marketing, sports, law, the military or the performing arts, but any high-level executive or directorial role would make good use of their skill set.

CHINESE ASTROLOGY

Health

The active and energetic Tiger usually shakes off the inconvenience of minor illnesses with a flick of the tail, but should make time to stop to avoid risk of burnout.

Independent to the point of being a loner, deep down the Tiger needs love and support to ward off low mood, so is advised to cultivate some close relationships.

Walking in nature will also lift a Tiger's spirits and provide much-needed breathing space in a high-speed life.

Influence over other signs

The year of the Tiger can feel exciting and unpredictable, as if anything could and might happen.

This can be stimulating for signs that love a bit of adventure, but quite scary and unsettling for calmer signs that prefer a steadier rhythm.

Either way, it is an expansive time and won't be boring!

The Rabbit

RABBIT YEARS

6 February 1951 – 25 January 1952: **Metal**
25 January 1963 – 12 February 1964: **Water**
11 February 1975 – 30 January 1976: **Wood**
29 January 1987 – 16 February 1988: **Fire**
16 February 1999 – 4 February 2000: **Earth**
3 February 2011 – 22 January 2012: **Metal**
22 January 2023 – 9 February 2024: **Water**
8 February 2035 – 27 January 2036: **Wood**

COLOURS: Pink, Red, Purple, Blue

NUMBERS: 3, 4 and 6

FIXED ELEMENT: Wood

Traits

The Rabbit is smart, gentle, kind and affectionate, and prefers to avoid conflict if at all possible. As such, they have strong diplomatic skills and a canny knack of self-preservation.

Intuitive, sensitive and empathetic, Rabbits are cultured and artistic, while undeniably reserved and unassuming.

Steering clear of confrontation can lead to charges of weakness, but the wily Rabbit knows what it's doing and how to play the long game.

CHINESE ASTROLOGY

Relationships

Security and stability are watchwords for the Rabbit in relationships, and they are happiest with positive partners who aren't averse to compromise as a route to harmony.

One of the quieter signs, Rabbits are well-suited to Goats and Pigs who are equally loving and gentle. They are less compatible with a Rooster, Horse or Rat.

Highly sociable, Rabbits are great company and wise, supportive friends.

Career

Intellectual, imaginative and sophisticated, Rabbits are clever communicators and their negotiating skills are highly prized.

Although quiet and not naturally drawn to leadership roles, their diligence leads to results, and they work well as counsellors, mediators, teachers and academics, lawyers, designers, medical practitioners and administrators, and at creative jobs in the arts or fashion.

Health

Provided they can avoid stressful situations – which is one of their key skills after all – Rabbits generally enjoy good health and longevity among the signs.

They are sensitive creatures, but usually well-disciplined and good at taking time out to recover from any physical or emotional illness.

Rabbits like to take it easy and enjoy the good things in life, so need to build exercise into their routine and avoid any over-indulgence that might place strain on their Wood element's associated organ of the liver.

Influence over other signs

Rabbit years are a moment of calm between the excitement and volatility of Tiger and Dragon years.

They are good times to practise compassion and diplomacy to resolve differences, but may be a little frustrating for signs who prefer to live life at a faster pace.

The Dragon

DRAGON YEARS

26 January 1952 – 13 February 1953: **Water**

13 February 1964 – 31 January 1965: **Wood**

31 January 1976 – 17 February 1977: **Fire**

17 February 1988 – 5 February 1989: **Earth**

5 February 2000 – 23 January 2001: **Metal**

23 January 2012 – 9 February 2013: **Water**

10 February 2024 – 28 January 2025: **Wood**

28 January 2036 – 14 February 2037: **Fire**

COLOURS: Gold, Silver, Grey-White

NUMBERS: 1, 6 and 7

FIXED ELEMENT: Earth

Traits

Generally considered to be the most powerful sign of the zodiac, the Dragon is confident, enthusiastic, charismatic and tenacious.

A resourceful and authoritative attitude, along with a large ego, propels a Dragon toward its goals, and it likes to lead the way.

However, despite also being intelligent, brave and ambitious, Dragons must guard against impatience and too much self-reliance, which can lead to folly.

Relationships

The attractive and self-confident Dragon is easy to fall in love with and makes a good pairing for many of the other signs, but is deemed most compatible with the Rat, Monkey, Tiger and Snake.

Least likely to gel are a Dragon and a Dog, with each finding it hard to make the necessary compromises to be together.

Positive and self-sufficient, Dragons may not need many friends, but if they are on your side, they are dependable, fierce and have your back.

Career

Dragons relish work they can get their teeth into, and are happiest embracing challenges and taking risks.

Entrepreneurial and innovative, they work hard, and expect and achieve results. They are drawn to CEO/leadership roles, but their "take no prisoners" approach can cause friction.

Suitable careers include politics, law, banking, the military, medicine, engineering, advertising and the performing arts.

Health

Dragons thrive on their busy, active and varied lifestyle, and benefit from a general lack of anxiety bolstered by their self-belief.

Their forceful, full-throttle nature will benefit from the balancing influence of gentler forms of exercise and self-care, such as yoga, tai chi or regular meditation.

THE 12 ANIMAL SIGNS

Influence over other signs

The word for a Dragon year is "adventure", which is exhilarating for some and terrifying for others!

The high-octane, driving energy of the sign brings change, which can sometimes teeter towards chaos.

Hold your nerve, buckle up and come along for the ride!

The Snake

SNAKE YEARS

14 February 1953 – 2 February 1954: **Water**

1 January 1965 – 20 January 1966: **Wood**

18 February 1977 – 6 February 1978: **Fire**

6 February 1989 – 25 January 1990: **Earth**

24 January 2001 – 11 February 2002: **Metal**

10 February 2013 – 30 January 2014: **Water**

29 January 2025 – 16 February 2026: **Wood**

15 February 2037 – 3 February 2038: **Fire**

COLOURS: Black, Red, Yellow

NUMBERS: 2, 8 and 9

FIXED ELEMENT: Fire

Traits

Watchful, wise and intuitive, the Snake is a sophisticated and enigmatic sign that gives little away.

Guarded and discreet, but strategic and calculating, Snakes are intensely private, but also friendly and likeable.

People are generally drawn to Snakes, but treat them with care as they can exhibit flashes of jealousy or temper. They are excellent at discovering secrets and use the knowledge they gather to further their own cause.

CHINESE ASTROLOGY

Relationships

The mysterious, mesmerizing and sensual Snake will nevertheless make a dedicated partner for the right person, once they have made their careful choice.

They are most compatible with a Rooster, Ox or Dragon, who have complementary characteristics but share the Snake's determined nature. They are least well-matched with a Pig.

Snakes are equally discerning when choosing friends and tend to have a smaller circle than most.

Career

Smart and focused, with a logical mind and an eye for detail, Snakes are deep thinkers, fast learners and good problem-solvers.

They work well in finance, law, medicine, science and politics, but can also excel in creative careers in the arts, fashion and entertainment.

Confident, charming and self-sufficient, Snakes are generally very successful at achieving their goals.

CHINESE ASTROLOGY

Health

Snakes like a quiet, well-ordered life and anything that upsets this can cause a stress reaction.

The Snake's fixed element of Fire is associated with the heart, so Snakes should pay particular attention to heart health and keeping any stress under control.

Regular gentle, relaxing exercise, such as swimming, tai chi or yoga, are excellent ways for Snakes to maintain equilibrium.

THE 12 ANIMAL SIGNS

Influence over other signs

As the first zodiac sign, the Year of the Snake may be as beguiling and mysterious as the sign itself, with progress hard to measure among prevailing energies of secrecy and subterfuge.

It's a good time to make connections and build relationships – just remember not to take everything on trust.

The Horse

HORSE YEARS

3 February 1954 – 23 January 1955: **Wood**

21 January 1966 – 8 February 1967: **Fire**

7 February 1978 – 27 January 1979: **Earth**

26 January 1990 – 13 February 1991: **Metal**

12 February 2002 – 31 January 2003: **Water**

31 January 2014 – 18 February 2015: **Wood**

17 February 2026 – 5 February 2027: **Fire**

4 February 2038 – 23 January 2039: **Earth**

COLOURS: Red, Green, Yellow

NUMBERS: 2, 3 and 7

FIXED ELEMENT: Fire

Traits

High-spirited, energetic and enthusiastic, the Horse is an open and fun-loving sign always seeking the next adventure.

Horses love being the centre of attention – they are quick-witted and great company – but their independent and restless nature means they like to forge their own path and dislike being tied down.

A horse should be aware of its impulsive streak and take a moment to look around before galloping on to the next project.

Relationships

Passionate and frequently falling in love, the Horse can be hard to tame and jealously guards its freedom.

Horses are most compatible with the strong and secure, but equally gregarious, signs of the Tiger and the Dog, but also match well with the easy-going Goat.

Rats and Snakes tend not to pair well with Horses as these relationships are often characterized by mutual inflexibility.

Career

Not afraid of hard work, the Horse is a good communicator and motivational leader. Ambitious and extroverted, they prefer to be in charge and don't like taking orders.

Jobs that use their sharp mind and involve interaction with others suit them best, and good career choices include journalism, communications and PR, advertising, hospitality, sports player or coach, tour guide or artist/performer.

CHINESE ASTROLOGY

Health

Often a lover of physical exercise,
the Horse is a generally healthy,
active and robust creature.

Their positive mental attitude goes
a long way to supporting good health,
but Horses must take care to heed
any warning signs of illness and
not brush them off.

Invigorating exercise, such as running
or team sports, suits the sociable
Horse as too much time cooped up or
alone can lead to stress, but this should
be moderated by some gentle exercise
to strike a healthy balance.

Influence over other signs

Change and turbulence are common aspects of the Year of the Horse, and these suit some signs more than others.

Opportunities for progress abound, but for the more risk-averse animals, steadiness and perseverance should counteract any volatility they find too overwhelming.

The Goat

GOAT YEARS

24 January 1955 - 10 February 1956: **Wood**

9 February 1967 - 28 January 1968: **Fire**

28 January 1979 - 15 February 1980: **Earth**

14 February 1991 - 2 February 1992: **Metal**

1 February 2003 - 20 January 2004: **Water**

19 February 2015 - 7 February 2016: **Wood**

6 February 2027 - 25 January 2028: **Fire**

24 January 2039 - 11 February 2040: **Earth**

COLOURS: Brown, Red, Purple

NUMBERS: 2 and 7

FIXED ELEMENT: Earth

Traits

Calm, kind, creative and artistic, the Goat is a gentle sign liked by pretty much everybody due to its compassionate and nurturing character.

Goats can be thought of as pushovers and, indeed, they often do anything to avoid an argument, but they actually have great resilience and inner strength and very much know their own minds.

CHINESE ASTROLOGY

Relationships

Sensual, affectionate and caring, the Goat is most compatible with the other sweet-tempered and cultured signs of the Rabbit and the Pig.

It pairs least well with a Dog or Ox, as these matches struggle to really understand each other.

Easy-going and generous, Goats love company and make excellent hosts, always ensuring their friends are having a good time.

THE 12 ANIMAL SIGNS

Career

Strong team players, Goats like to work in a supportive, creative environment and impart a sense of calm to those around them. They are good at building relationships and will advance along their chosen path despite their quiet compliant nature.

Artistic careers that make use of their imagination suit them well, such as interior design, painting, writing, filmmaking, gardening or architecture, as well as caring professions, including nursing or social work.

CHINESE ASTROLOGY

Health

The Goat's calm approach to life helps minimize their stress, which serves as a major boost to their overall health and wellbeing.

They should take care, however, that this calmness doesn't slide into inactivity or exercise that is too gentle!

Swimming and active yoga or Pilates would be particularly good for Goats, alongside a healthy diet and regular mealtimes to support the organs associated with the Earth element – the stomach and spleen.

THE 12 ANIMAL SIGNS

Influence over other signs

Following the volatile Year of the Horse, a Goat year is a much steadier, quieter place that gives space for some calm and consolidation.

Busy, active signs should take the opportunity to catch their breath, and the generally slower pace gives everyone the chance to stop, heal and appreciate the gentler things in life.

The Monkey

MONKEY YEARS

11 February 1956 – 29 January 1957: **Fire**

29 January 1968 – 15 February 1969: **Earth**

16 February 1980 – 4 February 1981: **Metal**

3 February 1992 – 21 January 1993: **Water**

21 January 2004 – 8 February 2005: **Wood**

8 February 2016 – 27 January 2017: **Fire**

26 January 2028 – 12 February 2029: **Earth**

12 February 2040 – 31 January 2041: **Metal**

COLOURS: White, Blue, Gold

NUMBERS: 4 and 9

FIXED ELEMENT: Metal

Traits

Clever and mischievous in equal measure, the Monkey is as cheeky as its common epithet describes.

Its playful, gregarious personality makes it an entertaining companion, but be aware that a Monkey will always put itself first and can have a devious streak that it's happy to employ in pursuit of its goals.

That said, the Monkey's love of life is infectious, and their inventive, imaginative and inquisitive nature stimulates those around them.

Relationships

Fun-loving and sociable, it's easy to be charmed by a Monkey, but their deep-seated fear of being bored, coupled with their impulsive nature, means it can take a while before they settle down with their ideal partner.

Rats and Dragons match best with Monkeys as similarly spirited signs who share the same goals.

The competition between a Monkey and a Tiger, however, makes this the least compatible pairing.

THE 12 ANIMAL SIGNS

Career

Hard-working and highly adaptable, the Monkey will make a success of any job that uses its brain, charm and confident patter. For this reason, jobs in sales, communications, trading and finance suit Monkeys well.

Their sharp minds also work well with careers in law, science and medicine, and their energy and outgoing nature lend themselves to sports, teaching and performing roles, too.

CHINESE ASTROLOGY

Health

The active, forward-facing Monkey is generally a healthy and positive individual, but they must take care to avoid over-stimulation which can lead to anxiety.

The main organs associated with the Monkey's fixed element of Metal are the lungs, so taking time to rest and to practise slower, more repetitive physical activity will be beneficial.

Meditation and breathing exercises will also help to quieten the busy mental chatter.

THE 12 ANIMAL SIGNS

Influence over other signs

A Monkey year brings excitement with a side order of unpredictability.

Signs and characters that love a bit of risk can thrive on this energy and capitalize on new opportunities, while others may prefer to exercise a degree of caution with new projects and relationships.

The Rooster

ROOSTER YEARS

30 January 1957 – 17 February 1958: **Fire**

16 February 1969 – 5 February 1970: **Earth**

5 February 1981 – 24 January 1982: **Metal**

22 January 1993 – 9 February 1994: **Water**

9 February 2005 – 28 January 2006: **Wood**

28 January 2017 – 15 February 2018: **Fire**

13 February 2029 – 2 February 2030: **Earth**

1 February 2041 – 21 January 2042: **Metal**

COLOURS: Gold, Brown, Yellow

NUMBERS: 5, 7 and 8

FIXED ELEMENT: Metal

Traits

Popular, dependable and warm-hearted, the self-aware Rooster is efficient, confident and ambitious.

Roosters strive for excellence with their precise approach to life that sometimes borders on perfectionism.

Plain-speaking and occasionally bossy, this sign is nevertheless thoughtful and loyal, and makes a devoted friend who will always have your best interests at heart.

Relationships

Flamboyant, passionate and sometimes sensitive, the Rooster can be hard to get to know well, but their steadiness and dedication make for a reliable life partner.

Best matched with the similarly determined Snake or Ox, a Rooster is least compatible with a Rabbit, who can feel intimidated by their frank comments, or with another Rooster who would compete with them to rule the roost.

Career

With excellent organizational capabilities and a phenomenal ability to multi-task, the smart Rooster is highly capable of achieving its goals.

Its plate-spinning prowess fits well with any self-employed line of work, and a flair for creativity bodes well for success in high-level planning and administrative roles.

Roosters also do well in public-facing careers – including broadcast journalism, hospitality, teaching and music – as well as those where detail is important, such as accounting and finance.

Health

The Rooster is a busy sign, up early and rarely sitting still, and this active lifestyle generally promotes good health and wellbeing.

However, Roosters can be prone to over-indulgence and should practise moderation in all things.

Their perfectionism can also trigger bouts of stress and anxiety, so they are advised to use their legendary self-discipline to schedule in regular exercise. This should sometimes be strenuous, to use up excess energy, and sometimes gentle – yoga and tai chi are always good – to bring peace and calm.

THE 12 ANIMAL SIGNS

Influence over other signs

The Year of the Rooster is an optimistic time when this sign's vivacity comes to the fore.

New trends may be set, but hard work is required to be able to capitalize on the year's creative energy.

Consistency is key, but try to avoid getting bogged down in too much detail.

The Dog

DOG YEARS

2 February 1946 – 21 January 1947: **Fire**

18 February 1958 – 6 February 1959: **Earth**

6 February 1970 – 25 January 1971: **Metal**

25 January 1982 – 12 February 1983: **Water**

10 February 1994 – 30 January 1995: **Wood**

29 January 2006 – 16 February 2007: **Fire**

16 February 2018 – 4 February 2019: **Earth**

3 February 2030 – 22 January 2031: **Metal**

COLOURS: Green, Red, Purple

NUMBERS: 3, 4 and 9

FIXED ELEMENT: Earth

Traits

Reliable, caring and protective, the Dog is loyal, honest and a lot of fun.

Dogs are happiest as part of a group (or pack) and will defend their friends at all costs.

Trustworthy and straightforward, they feel injustice keenly, but can sometimes be inflexible – even argumentative – and
slow to change their mind.

Relationships

Trust is of utmost importance to a Dog – it can take time to earn a Dog's trust but, once given, they are faithful and affectionate partners.

Deeply moral creatures, they abhor any kind of deception and expect their mates to treat them with equal respect.

Good-natured and outgoing, they are best paired with a Tiger or a Horse, who share their inquisitive nature and love of life. They are least well-matched with a Dragon, with both signs' stubbornness a likely issue.

Career

Good as a team player or a calm, unselfish leader, a Dog tends to be highly valued wherever they work.

They are helpful, discrete and driven to be of service to others, so careers in social work, law, diplomacy, medicine, education and care work suit them well.

In addition, their strong trait of trustworthiness lends itself well to working with finances in any organization.

Health

Generally strong and active creatures, Dogs thrive on regular exercise and benefit from participating in group activities more than sole pursuits.

The stomach and digestive system are associated with the Dog's fixed element of Earth, so an excess of fatty or processed foods should be avoided.

Although usually pretty stoic, Dogs can be prone to bouts of pessimism, which trigger anxiety and other stress-related issues. Mood-boosting exercise, such as swimming or walking in nature, will help.

THE 12 ANIMAL SIGNS

Influence over other signs

The prevailing energy in any Year of the Dog is one of caring, for others and the world, as well as nurturing and supporting close relationships.

It is a time of opportunity and the completion of projects through diligence and hard work, but the focus on home, family and security may feel stifling for some.

The Pig

PIG YEARS

22 January 1947 – 9 February 1948: **Fire**

7 February 1959 – 27 January 1960: **Earth**

26 January 1971 – 14 February 1972: **Metal**

13 February 1983 – 1 February 1984: **Water**

31 January 1995 – 18 February 1996: **Wood**

17 February 2007 – 6 February 2008: **Fire**

5 February 2019 – 24 January 2020: **Earth**

23 January 2031 – 10 February 2032: **Metal**

COLOURS: Yellow, Grey, Brown, Gold

NUMBERS: 2, 5 and 8

FIXED ELEMENT: Water

THE 12 ANIMAL SIGNS

Traits

Easy-going, trusting and compassionate, the Pig is a kind and patient friend who likes to have a good time.

Pigs like their luxuries but are happy to share them, which makes them a very popular sign!

They are hard-working and tenacious – to the point of being literally pig-headed at times – but are always looking to make the world a more harmonious place.

CHINESE ASTROLOGY

Relationships

The sensual and sensitive Pig makes a loving and committed partner, and one best-suited to a respectful and affectionate mate who will not take them for granted.

They are most compatible with either a Rabbit or a Goat, who share their caring and artistic nature. Pigs are least compatible with Snakes, with whom they can struggle to communicate effectively.

Career

Methodical and self-disciplined, Pigs are hard-working and always get the job done.

Known for being good with people, they are not overly ambitious and are content to progress at a steady rate in their chosen field.

Often drawn to work for the public good, the Pig will do well in the fields of teaching, law, medicine, social work, HR and customer service, design, hospitality, art and music.

CHINESE ASTROLOGY

Health

The sturdy Pig has a generally strong constitution, but needs to take care not to over-indulge in too much rich food.

Water is their fixed element, associated with the kidneys and bladder, so maintaining good hydration is essential.

Pigs can be prone to health anxiety, which is best combated by regular exercise. A good variety is key, as it will keep the Pig mentally as well as physically stimulated.

Influence over other signs

The final year in a 12-year cycle, the Year of the Pig is a good time for housekeeping and completion of projects.

Its over-arching energy is stability and community, but also expectation ahead of the cycle starting again.

Some signs will achieve their long-standing goals in a Pig year, while others will hunker down and enjoy time with friends and family.

> **It does not matter how slowly you go, as long as you do not stop.**
>
> Confucius